WORLD ALMANAC LIBRARY OF THE MIDDLE EAST

30.60/22.85 ea. All 6 for 183.60/137.10

Accelerated Reader Disk: AR Quizzes Available

This series provides the background and context students need to understand today's headlines about one of the worlds most important and volatile regions.

WORLD ALMANAC, Grades 5-12, 2007, 48 Pages, 7" x 9 1/4", color photos, Glossary, Charts, Maps, Primary source quotations and Timelines.

GEOGRAPHY

CONFLICTS OF THE MIDDLE EAST - Downing, David

GEOGRAPHY AND RESOURCES OF THE MIDDLE EAST - Downing, David

GOVERNMENTS AND LEADERS OF THE MIDDLE EAST - Downing, David

HISTORY OF THE MIDDLE EAST - Downing, David

PEOPLES AND CULTURES OF THE MIDDLE EAST - Barber, Nicola

RELIGIONS OF THE MIDDLE EAST - Stacey, Gill

HISTORY
of the Middle East

David Downing

Academic Consultant:
William Ochsenwald
Professor of History, Virginia Polytechnic Institute
and State University

WORLD ALMANAC® LIBRARY

Please visit our website at: www.garethstevens.com
For a free color catalog describing World Almanac® Library's list of high-quality books
and multimedia programs, call 1-800-848-2928 (USA) or 1-800-387-3178 (Canada).
World Almanac® Library's Fax: (414) 332-3567.

Library of Congress Cataloging-in-Publication Data

Downing, David, 1946-
    History of the Middle East / David Downing.
      p. cm. — (World Almanac Library of the Middle East)
    Includes bibliographical references and index.
    ISBN-10: 0-8368-7336-X — ISBN-13: 978-0-8368-7336-8 (lib. bdg.)
    ISBN-10: 0-8368-7343-2 — ISBN-13: 978-0-8368-7343-6 (softcover)
    1. Middle East—History—Juvenile literature. I. Title. II. Series.
    DS62.D68   2006
    956—dc22   2006014031

First published in 2007 by
World Almanac® Library
A Member of the WRC Media Family of Companies
330 West Olive Street, Suite 100
Milwaukee, WI 53212, USA

Produced by Discovery Books
Editors: Geoff Barker, Amy Bauman, Paul Humphrey, and Gianna Quaglia
Series designer: Sabine Beaupré
Designer and page production: Ian Winton
Photo researcher: Rachel Tisdale
Maps: Stefan Chabluk
Academic Consultant: William Ochsenwald,
    Professor of History, Virginia Polytechnic Institute and
    State University
World Almanac® Library editorial direction: Mark J. Sachner
World Almanac® Library editor: Alan Wachtel
World Almanac® Library art direction: Tammy West
World Almanac® Library production: Jessica Morris

Photo credits: cover: David W. Hamilton/Image Bank/Getty Images; p. 5: Andrea
Pistolesi/The Image Bank/Getty Images; p. 6: Art Directors and Trip; p. 9: The Art
Archive/CORBIS; p. 10: Hulton Archive/Getty Images; p. 11: Hulton-Deutsch
Collection/CORBIS; p. 13: Keystone/Getty Images; p. 15: Carl Mydans/Time Life
Pictures/Getty Images; p. 17: Keystone/Getty Image; p. 18: Central Press/Getty Images;
p. 20: Three Lions/Getty Images; p. 23: Ted Thai/Time Life Pictures/Getty Images; p. 25:
Karl Schumacher/AFP/Getty Images; p. 27: Joseph Barrak/AFP/Getty Images; p. 29: Kaveh
Kazemi/Keystone/Getty Images; p. 31: Robert Nickelsberg/ Time Life Pictures/Getty Images;
p. 33: Romeo Gacad/AFP/Getty Images; p. 34: Department of Defense; p. 37: Per-Anders
Pettersson/Getty Images; p. 39: Karim Sahib/AFP/Getty Images; p. 41: AFP/Getty Images;
p. 42: Ross Land/Getty Images

Printed in the United States of America

1 2 3 4 5 6 7 8 9 10 09 08 07 06

CONTENTS

Cover: Camels and tourists mingle under the ruins of the Great Colonnade in Palmyra, Syria. Palmyra was an important trading and cultural center in ancient times.

The Middle East

The term *Middle East* has a long and complex history. It was originally used by the British in the nineteenth century to describe the area between the Near East (those lands gathered around the eastern end of the Mediterranean Sea) and Britain's empire in India. This area included Persia (later Iran), the **Mesopotamian provinces** of the **Ottoman Empire** (later Iraq), and the eastern half of Saudi Arabia. It was centered on the Persian Gulf.

The British had separate military commands for the Near East and the Middle East, but between the two world wars these commands were joined together. The new Middle East

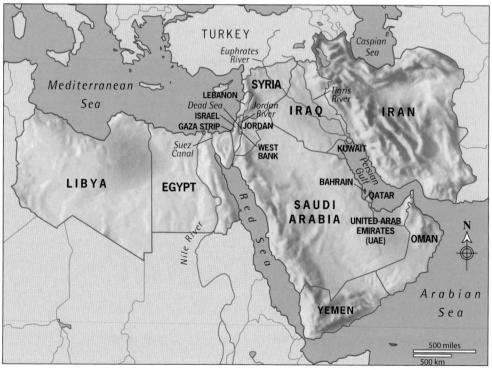

This map shows the fifteen countries of the Middle East that will be discussed in this book, as well as the West Bank and the Gaza Strip

The Western or "Wailing" Wall in Jerusalem is a retaining wall from the time of the Second Temple, which was destroyed in A.D. 70 by the Romans. The wall is sacred both to Jews and Muslims.

Command included the old Near East Command, and stretched from Iran to Libya. After World War II, the term Near East fell out of use. By the end of the twentieth century, the term Middle East was in general use, both outside and inside the region itself. In this series, it is taken to include fifteen countries: Libya and Egypt in north Africa; the Mediterranean coast states of Israel, Lebanon, and Syria; Jordan, Iraq, and Iran; and the Arabian Peninsula countries of Bahrain, Kuwait, Saudi Arabia, United Arab Emirates, Oman, Yemen, and Qatar. It also includes the Arab Palestinian territories of the Gaza Strip and the West Bank.

Why is this region important? Two reasons stand out. One, the Middle East was the original source of civilization, and the three great religions of **Christianity**, **Judaism**, and **Islam** all grew up there. The area includes Israel, the state of the Jewish people, and a significant proportion of the world's Muslims. Two, the Middle East has two-thirds of the fuel that keeps the rest of the world running—oil. For these two reasons alone, the affairs of the Middle East—its peoples and resources, religions and politics, revolutions and wars—are of vital interest to everyone on the planet.

This book looks at the history of the modern Middle East. After an introductory look at the region's pre-twentieth-century history, it examines in detail the major developments that have affected the region since World War I—the struggle to achieve independence, the failure of **Arab nationalism**, the turn to a political and social life more heavily influenced by Islam, and the rise of **terrorism**. In conclusion, the book assesses the current state of the Middle East and the choices facing its governments and peoples.

CHAPTER 1

From Ancient Times to 1920

Beginnings

Most historians place the beginnings of civilization in the Middle East. Settled agriculture started there around 6000 B.C. The first cities were built; writing was invented. The region would eventually give birth to all three of the great monotheistic, or "one-God," religions—Christianity, Judaism,

This famous building is the mosque of Abu Dulaf, in Iraq. It was built between A.D. 859 and 861.

The Birth of Islam

Islam was founded by the Prophet Muhammad in Arabia in the seventh century A.D. Muhammad was born in the city of Mecca (in present-day Saudi Arabia) around 570. According to his own testimony, he began, around the age of forty, to receive messages from God (known in Arabic as Allah). Muhammad's record of these messages became Islam's holy book, the Koran. Forced to leave Mecca in 622, Muhammad set up his religious community in Medina. In 630, he returned to Mecca as a conqueror. By his death in 632, he controlled most of the Arabian Peninsula. The written records of his sayings and daily behavior became known, respectively, as the *Hadith* and the *Sunna*. These, along with the Koran, form the main sources of guidance for his Muslim followers, who today number more than one billion.

and Islam. For thousands of years, the inhabitants of the Middle East believed that they lived at the center of the world.

Civilization spread outward from the Middle East, encouraging the growth of new kingdoms and empires. In the fourth century B.C., one of these empires—that of the Macedonian Alexander the Great—conquered most of the Middle East, spreading Greek culture throughout. Three hundred years later, the Romans conquered the region. Over the next seven hundred years, the people of the Middle East frequently found themselves ruled by outsiders.

Islam and the Arab Empire

All this changed in the seventh century. Inspired by the new religion of Islam, the people of the Arabian Peninsula launched a war of conquest. By the early years of the eighth century, the Arabs had created an empire that included the entire Middle East, North Africa, and Spain. This empire soon began breaking into semi-independent and independent parts, but the Islamic civilization that they all represented was—for the next five hundred years—one of the most advanced civilizations on the planet. Cities like Cairo, Baghdad, and Damascus were centers of learning and culture that Europe, still struggling to escape its **Dark Ages**, could not at the time hope to match.

The Middle East still suffered attacks from outside. From the eleventh century on, some European states mounted a series of military expeditions called the **Crusades**, which had the aim of recovering the Christian Holy Land from the Muslims—the followers of Islam. Some of these campaigns were successful, but only temporarily. The great Mongol invasions of the thirteenth century were much more devastating to the Middle East. At that time, the nomadic Mongol tribes, originally from an area in eastern Asia between China and Russia, raided and conquered territories in Asia, Russia, and Eastern Europe. Egypt was the only great center of Arab Islamic culture that was spared. This enormous setback occurred just as Europe was entering the **Renaissance**, a period of astonishing cultural and scientific progress. At this point, the Middle East began falling behind.

Ottoman Rule

People of Turkic origin had been moving west into present-day Ukraine, Iran, and Turkey since the eleventh century. In the late fourteenth century, one of these groups—the Ottoman Turks—began conquering an empire. By the end of the seventeenth century, they ruled much of southeast Europe and most of the

Sunnis and Shi'as

In the late seventh century, a dispute arose over how the political and spiritual leaders of the Muslim world should be chosen. One group believed that the leader should come from the Prophet Muhammad's own family, which was then represented by the descendants of his son-in-law, Ali. This group became the Shi'at Ali (party of Ali), and are now called Shi'as. The other group believed that the best leader should be chosen, regardless of his family history. Their name, Sunni, comes from the word *sunnah*, which means "custom" or "path," referring to those who follow Muhammad's tradition. In the early twenty-first century, there are about 90 million Shi'as, mostly in Iran and Iraq, and more than 900 million Sunnis.

The first Crusade was launched in 1096 and there followed over 250 years of European military campaigns in the Holy Land. This illustration shows the capture of Damietta, in Egypt, in 1219.

Middle East. Since they were Muslims, the Ottoman Turks did little to change the religious or cultural life of the Middle East. The empire's political leader, the sultan, also became the caliph, or spiritual leader, of many Muslims.

Between the sixteenth and nineteenth centuries, the rest of the world largely ignored the Middle East. With the opening up of new sea routes between Europe and eastern Asia, the old land routes through the Middle East declined in importance. And since there was nothing in the region itself that the rest of the world wanted, the Middle East became something of a global backwater.

The Suez Canal and Oil

All of this changed with the opening of the Suez Canal in 1869. This canal, which cut across Egypt to connect the Mediterranean and Red Seas, provided quicker access for ships sailing from Europe to anywhere in eastern Asia. It soon became the lifeline of the British and French Empires in southeast Asia. The Middle East was again important to outsiders.

This importance grew in leaps and bounds as two new facts gradually became apparent. First, the development of motor transportation (on land, at sea, and in the air) raised the importance of oil. Second, it soon became apparent that the Middle East had a large amount of this "black gold." In the early years of the twentieth century, as Britain made plans to switch from a coal-fired navy to a faster, more efficient oil-driven navy, the first oil wells were already being drilled in the Middle East.

Fatal Promises

Before World War I, Britain and France had supported Turkish rule in the Middle East. The Turks were strong enough to maintain stability but weak enough to let the British and French do what they wanted. But when Turkey joined World War I on the German side in October 1914, the British and French decided to split the Middle East between them.

The two European countries kept this plan a secret, however. The war was not yet won, and they wanted help from the Arabs and the Jews. The Arabs could help them fight the Turks. So the British promised the Arabs post-war independence, and they promised the Jews a national homeland in Palestine. Both promises were broken. Both have haunted the Middle East ever since.

New Masters

After World War I, the British and French implemented their secret plan. Britain had ruled Egypt in all but name since the 1880s and had huge influence over the supposedly independent government of Persia (now Iran). The British also established control of the Arabian side of the Persian Gulf. Unaware of the **oil reserves** beneath the sands there, the British

Arab workers lay an oil pipeline through the Khuzistan Desert plain of Iran in 1910. Their work is being monitored by a European official.

British troops pose for a photograph in Mesopotamia during World War I. After the war Mesopotamia became part of the new state of Iraq.

left the rest of the Arabian Peninsula to govern itself. Italy, which had joined the British, French, and Russian side in the middle of World War I, was allowed to keep Libya.

The rest of the old Ottoman Empire in Asia was divided between five potential countries. Through the **League of Nations**, the British were given **mandates** to rule Palestine, Transjordan, and Iraq; the French mandates to rule Syria and Lebanon. Both countries were supposed to prepare these territories for independence, but they seemed in little hurry to do so. Everywhere, as Turkish flags were lowered, British and French flags were raised.

The Balfour Declaration

In 1917, the British Foreign Minister Arthur Balfour wrote to Lord Rothschild, a prominent banker and member of the British Jewish community. In this letter, Balfour announced that the British government viewed "with favour the establishment in Palestine of a national home for the Jewish people," and would support its creation. He went on to promise that "nothing shall be done which may prejudice the civil and religious rights of existing non-Jewish communities in Palestine."

CHAPTER 2

The Struggle for Independence

Egypt, Iran, and Arabia

There was not much progress toward either genuine independence or **democracy** between the two World Wars. Although Egypt was officially granted independence during that time in 1922, the British High Commissioner in Cairo remained the single most powerful man in the country, and British troops guarded the Suez Canal. If Egypt's king or parliament defied British wishes too openly—by, for example, demanding that the officers in the

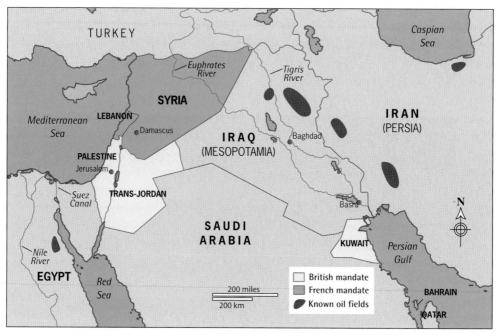

This map shows the British and French mandates as they were in 1939. Egypt had become independent in 1922, Saudi Arabia and Iraq in 1932.

A riot at Jaffa Gate, in Jerusalem, during a revolt in the British mandate of Palestine, January 1938.

Egyptian army be Egyptians rather than Britons—a Royal Navy warship would arrive to remind the Egyptians who was really in charge.

Persia was already independent in name, but there, too, the British played a key role, supporting the **shah**, Reza Pahlavi, in his campaign to **Westernize** the country in the 1930s, and then forcing him into exile when he proved too sympathetic to the Germans during World War II. The country was renamed Iran in 1935.

The British retained naval bases in the Persian Gulf and Yemen, but left the rest of the Arabian Peninsula alone. One Arab family, the House of Saud, took the opportunity to conquer all of the interior and much of the coast. The country of Saudi Arabia was proclaimed in 1932. Rather than invite the British in, the new country offered its first **oil concession** to the distant, less-threatening United States.

The Mandate Territories

In the mandate territories, little changed in the 1920s. Iraq was officially granted independence in 1932, but, as in Egypt, the British continued to hold real power behind the scenes. In Syria, Lebanon, and Transjordan, the lack of progress toward independence led to rising but manageable protests. In the territory of Palestine, however, events began spiralling out of control. In line with their promise of a "national home" for the Jews, the British allowed Jewish **immigration** to rise there. This angered the Arabs. But in line with the Balfour Declaration promise not to "prejudice the rights of existing non-Jewish communities," the British refused to allow unlimited immigration. This angered the Jews. Violence between Jews and Arabs increased.

Fighting in Palestine

After World War II, the violence in Palestine grew steadily worse. Both sides attacked each other, and some Jewish groups started a **guerrilla war** against the British, hoping to drive them out. Britain eventually directed the problem to the **United Nations (UN)**. The terrible sufferings of European Jews at the hand of the German Nazis during the war had increased worldwide support for the creation of a Jewish country, and in November 1947 the UN decided to partition the mandate territory. The partition plan was to create two smaller countries: one for the Arabs and one for the Jews. The Jews accepted the partition plan but the Arabs did not. Israel declared itself independent on May 14, 1948. On the following day, Arab armies from Egypt, Transjordan, Syria, Lebanon, and Iraq invaded in support of the Palestinian Arabs. The war lasted until early 1949, and ended with a comprehensive Israeli victory. The new state of Israel now occupied around 75 percent of the original mandate territory. Meanwhile Egypt took over the Gaza Strip, and Transjordan took over the West Bank.

Resentment of Outside Interference

As far as most Arabs were concerned, a new European colony had been planted in their midst. They blamed this state of affairs on two factors. The first was that their own governments

Palestinian Refugees

During the fighting in mandate Palestine (1947–1948) and during the war between Israel and the Arab countries that followed (1948–1949), about 725,000 Palestinian Arabs left their homes. Of these **refugees**, 470,000 ended up in the two regions of mandate Palestine that were not held by Israel—the Egyptian-controlled Gaza Strip and the Transjordan-controlled West Bank. Most of the rest of the people were divided fairly equally between Transjordan itself, Lebanon, and Syria. In all of these places, refugee camps were set up. The camps were supposed to be temporary, but many of them became the permanent homes of the Palestinian refugees.

were ineffective. The second was that the old **colonial** powers, which still stood behind these governments, prevented them from being effective. The answer to the central problem, many Arabs believed, was real independence. These Arab nationalists wanted to rule themselves and to **modernize** their countries.

Wherever they looked, the Arab and Iranian people saw evidence of continuing Western interference. British influence was still strong in Egypt, Iraq, and the Persian Gulf, and when the Iranian Prime Minister Mossadegh tried, in 1951–1953, to take full control of Iran's oil industry, the United States Central Intelligence Agency (CIA) arranged his overthrow. To both Arab and Iranian **nationalists**, this was all deeply humiliating.

Arab Nationalism

There were two well-known brands of Arab nationalism. **Ba'athism**—*Ba'ath* means "revival" or "renaissance"—was founded in Damascus, Syria, in the 1940s by Michel Aflaq. Ba'ath parties gained control of Iraq and Syria. **Nasserism** was named after Gamal Abdel Nasser, one of the Arab nationalist military officers who seized power in Egypt in 1952, and was president from 1956 to 1970. Nasser was the most important leader of the struggle for real independence, both in Egypt and the Arab world as a whole. Ba'athism and Nasserism shared the same basic ideals—they were both promodernization and pro-Arab unity, and they both opposed the West and Israel.

Mohammad Mossadegh pictured in 1953, the year he was deposed by the Shah of Iran, backed by the United States.

Gamal Abdel Nasser

Gamal Abdel Nasser (1918–1970), was a leading member of the Egyptian Free Officers who overthrew the government of King Farouk, in Egypt, in 1952. He served as prime minister from 1954 to 1956 and president from 1956 until his death in 1970. A committed Arab nationalist, Nasser used Soviet help to strengthen the Egyptian economy and armed forces and tried to create a United Arab Republic with Syria. After losing the 1967 war with Israel, the Six-Day War, he tried to resign, but huge demonstrations of support persuaded him to remain in office. Almost alone among Arab leaders, his popularity extended throughout the Arab world.

The Aswan High Dam and the Suez Crisis

The key element of Nasser's plan to modernize Egypt was the building of a dam on the Nile River at Aswan. This dam would generate large amounts of hydroelectricity and allow better control of the river, but it would be expensive. Nasser asked the United States to help him pay for the dam. At first, the United States agreed, but then the Americans decided not to contribute. Nasser decided that his only other source of funds was the Suez Canal. If he took over the canal, then Egypt—rather than its current owners, Britain and France—would be paid the **shipping tolls**. In June 1956, Egyptian troops occupied the **Canal Zone**.

The British and French were outraged. They persuaded the Israelis to launch an attack on the canal, and then landed their own troops in the Canal Zone, claiming that they had come only to keep the Israelis and Egyptians apart. No one believed them. The UN intervened on Egypt's side, forcing the British, French, and Israelis to withdraw. Nasser had won a great victory. Egypt, free of foreign troops, was truly independent at last.

Iraq

Two years later, in 1958, another group of Arab nationalist military officers seized power in Iraq. The pro-British royal

Egyptian prisoners are guarded by French soldiers as they sit on the beach of Fort-Fouad, Egypt, during the Suez crisis in 1956.

family and prime minister were killed. With this coup, Iraq also achieved genuine independence. The Iraqi Ba'ath Party had helped the military takeover but was soon cast aside. It would not come to power until 1968. In the meantime, all that remained of British influence in the Middle East were a few bases in the small kingdoms of the Arabian Peninsula.

Independence in North Africa

The Arab colonies of North Africa were also involved in struggles for independence from European colonial rule. Libya was an Italian colony until World War II and was granted independence in 1951. Tunisia and Morocco were French colonies, and the former saw some fighting between French troops and pro-independence fighters in the 1950s. The two countries were granted independence in 1955 and 1956.

Algeria, by contrast, was considered part of France. It had a large population of French colonists. These refused to accept separation from France and persuaded the French government to stand firm against Arab demands for independence. In 1954, a long and bitter war began, in which terrible atrocities were committed by both sides. In 1962, the French government finally agreed to Algerian independence.

CHAPTER 3

Arab Unity and War with Israel

Years of Arab Optimism

The ten years that followed Nasser's triumph in the Suez Crisis were years of Arab optimism. The Aswan High Dam became a symbol of Egyptian and Arab progress. It was, they hoped, the first of many giant steps along the road to economic development and prosperity. The merging of Egypt and Syria to form the United Arab Republic in 1958 provided a dramatic example of Arab unity. It seemed that the bad old days of foreign domination and economic backwardness were drawing to an end.

The success of the Arab nationalists created problems for the Arab **traditionalists**, or conservatives, who wanted things to stay much the way they were. These people still ruled most countries of

A picture taken in May 1964 shows the four huge hydraulic tunnels dug out of the rock, in the first stage of construction of the Aswan High Dam.

the Middle East, including all of the oil-rich Arabian countries. Knowing how popular nationalists like Nasser were with their own people, the conservative governments were quick to make nationalist gestures of their own. They helped support the Palestinian refugees. They gave economic aid to the oil-poor Arab states.

The oil producers also tried to get a better price for the growing volume of oil that they were selling to the richer countries of Europe, North America, and Japan. In 1960, they formed the Organization of Petroleum Exporting Countries (OPEC). The oil producers now began reaching agreement on how much oil each would sell, which gave them more control over the price that each could charge.

Dry Bread and an Onion

"If we want to have an idea of the way of life of our people, we should not look at the lights of Alexandria, Cairo, or Damascus. . . . We must look at the rural sector to know how the fellah [poor farmer] lives. He lives on wages in the service of a land-owner; as an agricultural laborer working four or five months a year and unemployed the rest of the year. He can scarcely find enough to eat, to subsist, for himself and his children. How does an itinerant agricultural worker live? He lives with the lowest wage a worker can get. Five years ago, I visited Kom Ombo [in southern Egypt] and the factories there. For lunch, each worker was eating dry bread and an onion—all of them the same. None of us can accept such living conditions."

President Nasser of Egypt, speaking in 1961. The need for economic development was always a crucial component of Arab nationalism. From Robert Stephens' Nasser *[New York: Penguin, 1971], 330.*

The United Arab Republic

The establishment of the United Arab Republic in 1958 was the Arab nationalists' first and only real attempt at putting their talk of Arab unity into practice. It involved a political union of Egypt and Syria. A central cabinet was set up, along with executive councils for the "Northern region" (Syria) and "Southern region" (Egypt). There was talk of Iraq and even Yemen joining up.

The Egyptian and Syrian leaders soon found themselves disagreeing about a wide range of policies, however, and in September 1961, the Syrians withdrew from the union. Egypt finally abandoned the name in 1971.

The Arab–Israeli War of 1967

As Arab optimism grew, only Israel reminded the Arab nations of their former weakness. The Arab nations continued to refuse to recognize the Jewish state, and small groups of fighters had launched largely unsuccessful raids across the borders, but Israel had survived and grown stronger. As the 1960s unfolded, nationalist leaders like Nasser began to believe that the Arab countries would soon be capable of reversing the defeat of 1948–1949.

The Israeli economy had two great strengths: a highly educated workforce and considerable financial support from abroad. It was developing much faster than the economies of the neighboring Arab countries. Israel's armed forces were better equipped and more highly motivated. They felt they had to be: few Israelis doubted that the Arabs meant to destroy them and to "drive them into the sea."

In the summer of 1967, Nasser grew more aggressive in his words and actions. He asked the UN to withdraw its troops from the Israeli-Egyptian border, and he closed the Straits of Tiran—Israel's only route to the east—to Israeli shipping. The Israelis didn't wait to see if he really intended war. They struck first. Surprise air attacks destroyed the Egyptian, Syrian, Jordanian, and Iraqi air forces on the ground. Lacking air support, the Arab ground forces lasted only six days. Israel took control of the Egyptian Sinai Peninsula, the Syrian Golan

Israeli Centurion tank corps prepare for battle during the Six-Day War in June 1967. Funding from the United States helped Israel build an extremely effective army and air force.

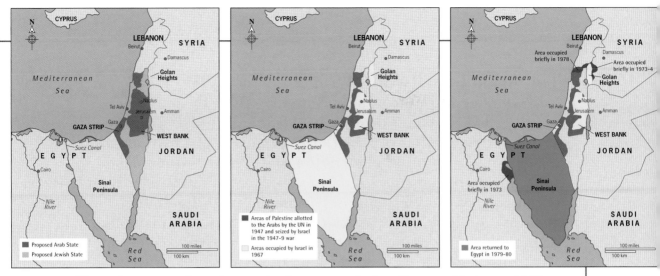

These three maps show changes in the areas under Israel's control between 1947 and 1980.

Heights, and those areas of the old mandate Palestine that it had not taken in 1948—the coastal Gaza Strip, the hills of the West Bank region, and East Jerusalem.

The Cost

The Arab–Israeli war of 1967, also known as the Six-Day War, proved costly for all concerned. Israel had defeated a threat to its survival and made future attacks more difficult by pushing back its borders. In the long run, however, the occupation of the West Bank and the Gaza Strip would prove to be a source of further conflict.

For the Palestinian Arabs, twenty years of waiting had proved in vain. Most now realized that the neighboring Arab countries would never win back Palestine. They would have to find their own ways of doing that. Over the following decades, they tried one method after another—guerrilla warfare, terrorism, **diplomacy**, and the street rebellion of the **intifada**.

For the Arab countries, 1967 proved worse than 1948. Some Arabs were willing to admit that the nationalists had proved just as ineffective as the old pro-Western governments they had replaced, but most were unwilling to abandon the nationalist dream. Egypt's Nasser was talked out of resigning, and other targets were found for blame. The most obvious was the United States, which gave such crucial financial and diplomatic support to Israel and had vetoed a UN resolution demanding that Israel withdraw the territories it had occupied.

The Arab–Israeli War of 1973

In November 1967, the United Nations passed Resolution 242, which called for Israel's withdrawal from occupied territories and Arab recognition of Israel's right to exist. But neither side was willing to act on it. The United States tried to get talks started but was not successful. Nasser decided that the only way of pushing the Israelis back across Sinai was to bomb their positions along the east bank of the Suez Canal. The Israelis responded by bombing Egyptian cities. When Nasser died in 1970, his successor Anwar Sadat reluctantly decided that there was only one thing that would shift the Israelis—a full-scale attack. The new Syrian president, Hafez Assad, agreed with him.

On October 6, 1973—the Jewish holy day of Yom Kippur—Egypt and Syria launched attacks across the Suez Canal and Golan Heights. Caught by surprise, the Israelis needed several days to recover. Once they did, however, the tide quickly turned. Nine days after the original Egyptian attack, Israeli forces were crossing the canal in the other direction, and driving into Egypt.

Two days after that, the Arab oil-producing countries announced that they were cutting back or halting their oil deliveries to the West. This, they hoped, would raise fears of a global **economic depression**, and put pressure on the United States. They assumed the United States would then put pressure on Israel—to accept a ceasefire and to leave the

Resolution 242

In November 1967, the United Nations Security Council unanimously passed Resolution 242. It called for
- the withdrawal of Israeli armed forces from occupied territories
- respect for the sovereignty, territorial integrity, and political independence of every state in the area, and their right to live in peace within secure and recognized boundaries, free from threats or acts of force
- a just settlement of the Palestinian refugee problem.

Anwar Sadat

Anwar Sadat (1918–1981) was a prominent member of the Egyptian Free Officers that overthrew the government of King Farouk in Egypt in 1952. Sadat served as Nasser's vice-president from 1964–1966 and 1969–1970 and succeeded him as president in 1970. He launched and lost the third Arab-Israeli War in 1973. After the defeat, he moved away from the Soviet Union and closer to the United States. He became the first leader of an Arab nation to reach a peace agreement with Israel in 1978 and was **assassinated** by an **Islamic fundamentalist** in 1981.

occupied territories. The Arabs were only partly correct. Israel accepted a ceasefire on October 24, but it refused to return any territory. Afraid that they were doing damage to their own economies, the Arab oil-producing states resumed prewar production rates and deliveries.

Despite success in the opening battles, the Arab nationalists had lost another war. Once again they blamed the United States, but this time they also disagreed among themselves over what to do next. The dreams of Arab unity were fading fast.

A "gasoline by appointment only" sign at a gas station in the United States during the oil shortage brought on by OPEC in the 1970s. The cost of gas rocketed as a result.

CHAPTER 4

Oil and the Cold War

In the years following World War II, Europe was divided into a democratic West, supported by the United States, and the **Communist** East, supported by the Soviet Union. Both countries sought to influence governments in other countries around the world, including those in the Middle East. The stand-off between them was known as the Cold War.

Israel

Israel's second decisive victory in six years made it more secure, but a lasting peace seemed as far away as ever. Most Israelis were unwilling to see the creation of a Palestinian Arab country. The government of Menachem Begin, which came to power in 1977, believed that the West Bank and the Gaza Strip were part of the ancient Land of Israel. They made no attempt to **annex** these areas, but they allowed the building of Israeli settlements in them. Israeli society became increasingly divided between those who wanted to trade land for peace and those who did not.

Arab Failure and Anger

For many Arabs, this second defeat offered evidence of the wider failure of Arab nationalism. But other problems in the region persisted. The Arabs had thrown off their old European masters,

The "Eisenhower Doctrine"

"The existing vacuum in the Middle East must be filled by the United States before it is filled by Russia."

President Dwight D. Eisenhower, speaking to the U.S. Congressional leaders in 1957, the year after the Suez Crisis. From Robert Stephens' Nasser *[New York: Penguin, 1971], 255.*

Egyptian President Sadat (left) shakes hands with Israeli Premier Begin as President Jimmy Carter looks on at Camp David, September 1978. As a result of these talks, a treaty granted recognition of Israel by Egypt, opened trade relations between the two countries, and limited Egyptian military build-up in the Sinai. Israel agreed to return the final portion of occupied Sinai to Egypt.

but it seemed as if the United States was now interfering in the Middle East as much as the Europeans had done. Arabs also thought they had set out on the path of political and economic development, but their governments were mostly **corrupt** and undemocratic, and their economies were making little headway.

The oil-poor countries like Egypt, Syria, Jordan, and Yemen were making much less economic progress than they had hoped. They were receiving some financial aid from the oil-rich countries, and some from the United States and the Soviet Union, both of whom wished to extend their influence in the region during the period of the Cold War. But it was not enough to overcome the region's natural disabilities such as its harsh environments and its lack of natural resources. On top of this, poor educational systems, poverty, and high unemployment were widespread.

The oil-rich countries were earning huge sums of money, but only a small number of people in these countries had any say over how the money was spent. In small Persian Gulf monarchies like Kuwait or Bahrain there was enough to go around, and even the poorest people received benefits like free education and health care. In the larger oil-rich countries—like Iran and Saudi Arabia—most ordinary people received little or no share of the wealth generated by oil. They watched as it disappeared into the pockets of a small elite group or was lavished upon modern weaponry and extravagant display. In the big cities and oil towns, local people saw foreigners flaunting Western attitudes toward sex and religion that many Muslims found offensive.

Arab Disunity

If Arab nationalism was not the answer to the Arabs' problems, then what was? There was no agreement. Arab unity, which had often seemed little more than a matter of words, was no longer even that.

Disagreements raged over what to do about Israel. In 1977, Egypt's President Sadat traveled to Jerusalem and addressed Israel's parliament. The following year, he recognized Israel's right to exist in exchange for the return of Sinai. He denied he was making a separate peace and abandoning Egyptian support of the Palestinians, but many people in the Arab world believed that he was. Egypt was thrown out of the **Arab League**.

As the hopes of Arab unity faded, **ethnic** and religious identities grew more important, threatening the national unity of several Middle Eastern countries. This threat was greatest in Lebanon, which was almost equally divided between Christian Arabs and Muslim Arabs. The arrival of many Palestinians in the early 1970s—most of whom supported the Muslims—worsened an already critical situation. In 1975, the country slid into a **civil war** that lasted for sixteen years.

The most basic disagreement, however, and

Creating Resentment

"It was the influx of hundreds and eventually thousands of American civilians and military personnel that created a level and type of foreign presence totally new to Iranians. Unlike invaders mounted on horses or imperialists carrying documents confirming territorial and economic cessions, the new aliens came to Iran to tend the machines of industrialization and war. Too few of the technologists knew or cared about Iranian culture. And too many, particularly those with limited education, took pride in calling highly developed Iranian culture 'camel culture' and deriding Iranians themselves as . . . 'rags,' 'stinkies,' and 'Bedouins'. . . .

"In October 1975, three American women clad in skimpy shorts and halters strode through the ancient Friday mosque talking and laughing while Muslims prayed. On other occasions, American teenagers drove motorbikes through the venerable Royal Mosque. . . . In city after city, month after month, other incidents great and small offended and enraged the Iranians."

American author Sandra Mackey. From The Iranians [Plume, 1998].

Ten years into the Lebanese civil war, rescuers try to save survivors in the Christian suburb of Beirut, Sin-el-Fil, in May 1986. It was the sixth car bomb attack in the Christian sector in five months.

the one that divided all of the Arab countries and (non-Arab) Iran, was over the value of the Westernization and modernization that both Arab nationalism and the shah's Iranian nationalism had represented. Now many Arabs believed these programs had failed both politically and economically. They argued that it was time to try something else, something better-suited to the Middle East and its Islamic values.

CHAPTER 5

Islamization

The Rise of Islamic Fundamentalism

The idea that religion and politics should be kept separate has been generally accepted in much of Europe and in North America for over two hundred years. The Arab nationalists also believed this. Leaders like Egypt's Nasser were Muslims, but their governments were not religious.

Old Light, New Light

"My brothers, you are the new light that will destroy the darkness of materialism [the desire to own more and more things]. You are the voices that echo the message of the Prophet Muhammad."

Hassan el-Banna, founder of the Egyptian Muslim Brotherhood, the first significant Islamic fundamentalist group in the modern Middle East. From David Downing's The Making of the Middle East *[Oxford: Heinemann Library, 2005].*

There had always been those in the Middle East who disagreed and did not believe that government and religion should be separate. They wanted their governments to reflect Islamic beliefs and to introduce Islamic policies. These people and the groups to which they belonged were often called Islamic fundamentalists. Some, like the Muslim Brotherhood in Egypt, attracted so much support that Arab nationalist governments found it necessary to ban them.

With the failure of Arab nationalism, more and more people began supporting the fundamentalists. Two crucial events—the Iranian Revolution of 1979 and the wars in Afghanistan (1979–1996)—increased the fundamentalists' power and influence throughout the Middle East.

Islamic Revolution in Iran

Throughout the 1960s and 1970s, the shah of Iran claimed that he was trying to modernize his country. This modernization, however, amounted to little more than buying modern weaponry for his armed forces and a few high-profile developments. There was no real democracy and no lasting economic development. For most Iranians, life got harder. As the gap between a small privileged class and the rest of the people widened, so resentment grew. Since the shah believed that Islam—Shi'a Islam, in Iran's case—was holding back the modernization of the country, he persecuted the **clergy** and sent his most prominent critic—**Ayatollah** Ruhollah Musavi Khomeini— into **exile**.

A group of the Ayatollah Khomeini's supporters demonstrate on the streets of Tehran in 1979. They were calling for the religious leader's return from exile.

Having antagonized both the modernizers—who wanted more democracy and fairness—and the traditionalists—who wanted a return to Islamic values and practice—the shah found himself relying more and more on his much-feared **security police**, called SAVAK. But the more people SAVAK arrested and tortured, the more opponents the shah found he had. In January 1979, he was finally driven from power by an overwhelmingly popular revolution. A few days later, Ayatollah Khomeini returned from exile.

Modernizers Versus Traditionalists

Once the shah was gone, the two groups that had overthrown him discovered that they had totally different visions for Iran's future. The modernizers wanted a more democratic, less pro-Western, modern country. The traditionalists wanted an **Islamic republic**. From 1980–1982, civil conflict raged between these groups. It was won by the traditionalists.

Ayatollah Khomeini

Ruhollah Musavi Khomeini was born in Persia in 1902. As a Shi'a Islamic scholar and teacher, he stressed the part that religion should play in everyday life, including politics. In the 1960s, his writings secured him the leadership of Iran's **radical** clergy and won him promotion to ayatollah, a title of respect. Already a bitter opponent of the shah's pro-Western policies, he became increasingly outspoken. Exiled from Iran in 1964, he spent fifteen years in Turkey, Iraq, and France. Tape recordings of his writings and speeches were smuggled into Iran, however, and played a major role in increasing opposition to the shah. After the shah's overthrow in 1979, Khomeini returned to guide and lead the new Islamic republic. Under his leadership, Iran fought a war against Iraq between 1980 and 1988. He also gave help to Islamic fundamentalist groups in other Muslim countries, most notably Lebanon and Afghanistan.

The Afghan Wars

In April 1978, after civil war had broken out, the Afghan Communists seized power. Their policies, which included improving education, **land reform**, and more rights for women, were intended to modernize the country. They faced violent opposition from those against such reforms, and particularly from the Islamic clergy. Groups of Islamic fundamentalist fighters—the *mujahedin*—took up arms against the government.

In 1979, as the country slid into civil war, the Soviet Union sent in troops. The Soviets' aim was to help the Afghan Communists, but their presence only encouraged greater opposition. It also persuaded the United States to offer increasing support to the fundamentalists.

Unable to defeat the *mujahedin*, the Soviets withdrew in 1989. The Americans ceased their support for the fundamentalists. But the war went on for several more years. The Afghan Communist government was finally toppled in 1992, but the fundamentalist groups then turned on each other. By 1996, they had all been defeated by a new and even more extreme fundamentalist group, the Taliban. The Taliban ruled Afghanistan from 1996 to 2001.

Taliban fighters pose on top of a tank at a base they have won near Kabul in February 1995.

The Spread of Islamic Fundamentalism

The Iranian Revolution offered encouragement to all Middle Eastern Muslims who wanted religious government. However, the Iranian leadership found it hard to exert any real influence beyond their own country. For one thing, they were Shi'a Muslims, and most Middle Eastern Muslims were Sunnis. For another, they were fully occupied for most of the 1980s with the war against Iraq.

A Declaration of War

"We—with God's help—call on every Muslim who believes in God and wishes to be rewarded to comply with God's order to kill the Americans and plunder their money wherever and whenever they find it. We also call on the Muslim *ulema* [religious leaders], leaders, youths, and soldiers to launch the raid on Satan's U.S. troops and the devil's supporters allying with them and to displace those who are behind them so that they may learn a lesson."

Declaration of War issued by Osama bin Laden, together with the leaders of the World Islamic Front for the Jihad Against the Jews and the Crusaders, in Afghanistan, February 23, 1998. From Rohan Gunaratna's Inside Al Qaeda *[Hurst and Co., 2002].*

The Afghan wars were another matter. The thousands of volunteers who came from all over the Middle East to fight against the Soviets were mostly Sunni Muslims. Those who survived went back to their own countries as victorious warriors of Islam. They had ejected one superpower, the Soviets, from one Islamic country, and they saw no reason why they could not eject the other, the United States, from their own countries.

Other Middle Easterners were inspired to take a more fundamentalist approach. Since their beginnings in the 1960s, the Palestinian resistance groups had been mostly **secular** in outlook, but in the 1980s and 1990s, fundamentalist groups like Hamas and Islamic **Jihad** found more and more recruits.

The Turn to Terrorism

Saudi Arabian Osama bin Laden eventually became the most famous of the foreign mujahedin who fought in Afghanistan. During his time in Afghanistan, he founded an organization called al-Qaeda ("the base"), with which he planned to continue the Islamic struggle elsewhere. Its members, almost all of whom were fellow-veterans of the Afghan wars, would fight for Islam wherever they were needed—in Kashmir, Chechnya, the Middle East. As a first priority, bin Laden sought to force all foreign troops out of Saudi Arabia—the Prophet Muhammad's homeland. His chosen method was terrorism. He would frighten the foreign governments into submission. Over the next decade, his followers launched attacks around the world, including the September 11, 2001, (or 9/11) attacks on the United States.

By the time of the 9/11 attacks, Osama bin Laden was back in Afghanistan, a guest of the ruling Taliban. Although the Taliban were overthrown by Western military forces in November 2001, in the first stage of the U.S.-led **War on Terrorism**, Osama bin Laden escaped, and al-Qaeda's campaign of terror has continued. Today, while bin Laden has many supporters in the Middle East, many other Middle Easterners, although they share his hatred of the West and Western ways, condemn his methods.

An Afghan fighter watches clouds of smoke rise in Tora Bora as U.S. warplanes bomb positions held by Osama bin Laden's al-Qaeda fighters on December 13, 2001.

CHAPTER 6

Saddam Hussein

The Rise of Saddam

In Iraq, the Ba'ath party seized power in 1968. Saddam Hussein was given control of the security police, and a year later he became vice-president. From this point on, he was the real ruler of the country, although he only became president in 1979. The Ba'athists were Arab nationalists, and during the 1970s, they concentrated on securing the country's economic independence and development. They **nationalized** the oil industry, set up new industries, and introduced better education and health care. The lives of most ordinary Iraqis improved.

Saddam and the Iraqi Ba'athists were not interested in democracy, however. Opponents of the regime were often

Saddam Hussein following his capture in Tikrit, Iraq, on December 13, 2003.

imprisoned, tortured, and killed. In foreign affairs, Saddam was determined to make Iraq the most powerful nation in the region and to show that the Arabs were capable of winning wars. Although he was a practicing Muslim, Saddam, like Nasser before him, believed in secular government.

The Iran–Iraq War

At the end of the 1970s, the Iranian Revolution—and the revolutionary Islamic politics that it threatened to export— was beginning to worry both the Western powers and their conservative supporters in the Middle East. Saudi Arabia and the Persian Gulf monarchies were particularly concerned. Saddam's secular Iraq, they all decided, could help them keep fundamentalist Iran in check. They helped by giving Iraq money and arms.

Saddam also had reasons of his own for confronting Iran. The Shi'a Iranians were stirring up trouble among the Shi'a majority in southern Iraq, threatening his country's unity. And Saddam was tempted by the wealth of the Iranian oil fields, which lay just across his southern border. This area of Iran was inhabited by Arabs, whom Saddam believed would welcome an Iraqi invasion. In September 1980, he made the terrible mistake of setting his forces in motion.

Halabja

"A yellowish cloud spread out from the center of the explosion and became a thin mist. The air became filled with a mixture of smells—'bad garlic,' 'rotten onions,' and 'bad apples.' Those who were very close to the bombs died almost instantly. Those who did not die instantly found it difficult to breathe and began to vomit. The gas stung their eyes, skin, and lungs. . . . Many suffered temporary blindness. Those who could not run from the growing smell, mostly the very old, the very young, died.

"Ahmad Muhammad, a Kurd recalled that day. 'My mother and father were burned; they just died and turned black.' Bashir Shemessidin testified: 'In our village, 200 to 300 people died. All the trees dried up. It smelled like something burned. The whole world turned yellow.'"

From a U.S. Senate foreign relations report on the gas-attack that Saddam's forces launched on the Iraqi Kurdish town of Halabja in 1988. As cited by Mical L. Sifry and Christopher Cerf, editors, The Iraq War Reader *[Touchstone, 2003].*

They were not welcomed. Within months, it was clear that the war was unwinnable, but Iran was unwilling to make peace with the aggressor. The slaughter was only finally halted in 1988, with both sides utterly exhausted. The Western powers and conservative Arab countries had done nothing to help stop it. As far as they were concerned, a war that weakened both Arab nationalism and Islamic fundamentalism was a dream come true.

The Gulf War and After

Saddam's war had bankrupted his country. He asked the rulers of Saudi Arabia and Kuwait for financial help, claiming that he had fought Iran at least partly on their behalf. When they refused, Saddam decided to seek compensation by force. In the summer of 1990, he invaded Kuwait, claiming that it really belonged to Iraq. Somewhat to his surprise, the world united against him. In early 1991, a UN coalition, headed by the United States and including some Arab countries, pushed the

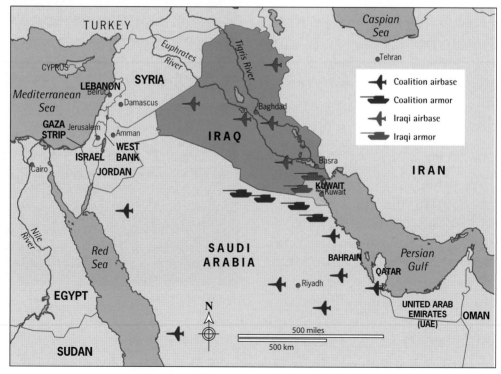

This map shows the Persian Gulf states and the distribution of military forces during the 1991 Gulf War.

Firefighters pull water hoses next to burning oil wells in Kuwait, seven months after the end of the Gulf War. Retreating Iraqi troops had smashed and torched 727 wells, polluting the atmosphere and creating crude oil lakes. Up to eight billion barrels of oil were spilled into the sea, damaging coastal areas up to 250 miles away.

Iraqi forces back out of Kuwait. Saddam's regime was allowed to survive, however. He was still needed as a counterbalance to revolutionary Iran, and any attack on Baghdad was considered to be too costly in terms of lives.

He remained a possible threat, however, and throughout the 1990s, great efforts were made to keep him relatively weak. **UN weapons inspectors** frequently searched Iraq for those **weapons of mass destruction** — nuclear, chemical, and biological — that Saddam had produced or tried to produce in the past. Fighting continued between Iraq's forces and the U. S. and British air forces that were permanently stationed in the area. **Economic sanctions** caused widespread suffering among ordinary Iraqis and widespread outrage in the rest of the Arab world. Saddam remained defiant, believing that Russia and France, each of which had trade and service contracts with Iraq, would veto any attempt by the UN Security Council to authorize an invasion of Iraq.

September 11, 2001, and the Overthrow of Saddam

Five months after the terrorist attacks on the World Trade Center and Pentagon, President George W. Bush gave his State of the Union address. In it, he identified Saddam Hussein's Iraq as part of an "Axis of Evil." Iraq was, he said, one of three nations hostile toward the United States and allegedly supporting terrorism. Though Saddam was no supporter of al-Qaeda, there was a genuine fear in the West that an alliance might be forged between the Iraqi dictator, who was known at one time to be developing weapons of mass destruction, and Osama bin Laden, who was known to want to lay his hands on such weapons.

Saddam had openly flouted UN resolutions demanding that he allow weapons inspectors to enter suspected weapons sites. In 1998, he forced the inspectors out of Iraq, only allowing them to return in late 2002, when an attack by the United States and its allies appeared imminent.

Supporters of the invasion of Iraq cite these facts, and the murderous nature of Saddam's regime, as the main reasons why the attack was justified. Others wonder whether an additional motive

Axis of Evil

"We must prevent the terrorists and regimes who seek chemical, biological, or nuclear weapons from threatening the United States and the world . . . Some of these regimes have been pretty quiet since September the eleventh. But we know their true nature. North Korea is a regime arming with missiles and weapons of mass destruction . . . Iran aggressively pursues these weapons and exports terror . . . Iraq continues to flaunt its hostility toward America and to support terror . . .

"States like these, and their terrorist allies, [make up] an Axis of Evil, arming to threaten the peace of the world. By seeking weapons of mass destruction, these regimes pose a grave and growing danger. They could provide these arms to terrorists. . . . They could attack our allies or attempt to blackmail the United States.

"I will not wait on events, while dangers gather. I will not stand by, as peril draws closer and closer. The United States of America will not permit the world's most dangerous regimes to threaten us with the world's most destructive weapons."

President George W. Bush, **State of the Union address,** *January 29, 2002.*

United Nations weapons inspectors return to their headquarters in Baghdad in 1997, after Iraq blocked them from entering weapons sites for the ninth time in ten days.

was the Western powers' desire to bring Iraq's huge oil reserves under Western control, in the face of growing instability across the oil-rich Middle East.

The Violent Aftermath

The invasion in March 2003 was an apparent success. Saddam's armies put up little resistance, and the **dictator** himself was eventually caught. But aerial bombing did enormous damage to an Iraqi economy already weakened by decades of war and sanctions, and life for ordinary Iraqis grew steadily worse. Three years after the invasion, power supplies had not been fully restored.

The occupation forces and their Iraqi allies (some of them returning exiles) found themselves facing increasing armed resistance from a wide range of opponents. Some were Saddam loyalists; others—like the group al-Qaeda in Iraq—were foreign fundamentalists, drawn to Iraq by the chance to fight the Western powers. Some were Sunnis who saw little future for themselves in an Iraq now dominated by the Shi'a majority. Others were ordinary Iraqis who had hated Saddam but who hated their foreign occupiers just as much. They killed many more civilians than foreign soldiers in their frequent attacks. On the plus side, a new constitution was agreed upon in 2005, and national elections were held early in 2006. There was, however, little sign of an end to the **insurgency**.

CHAPTER 7

The Middle East Today

Half a century has now passed since Nasser defied the British and French over the Suez Canal, and the ambitions of Arab nationalism remain unfulfilled. Economic development has been patchy, political development is almost nonexistent, and foreigners still have a great deal of influence in the region. The Middle East is riddled with conflicts, both between and inside its countries. The world's major source of oil has become its major generator of terrorism.

Israel and Iran

Iran's Islamic revolution is now more than a quarter of a century old. In the 1990s, after Ayatollah Khomeini's death, the Iranian government relaxed its strict rules. If it wished to participate in the global economy, it realized, then it had to be prepared to compromise. Since then—and since George W. Bush's inclusion of Iran in what he called the "Axis of Evil"— Iran's hard-line fundamentalists have made a comeback. There is much discontent over Iran's poor economic performance, but it seems likely that any foreign attack would unite most Iranians behind their government.

Israel has survived and, in many ways, prospered. The continuing occupation of Palestinian lands has, however, widened divisions within Israeli society and made that society less secure. Many believe the removal of settlements from the Gaza Strip will achieve little if the far greater number of settlements on the West Bank are allowed to remain. The possibility of conflict with Iran remains. Israel, which possesses nuclear weapons, has already said that it will take military action to prevent Iran from manufacturing them.

The Arab Middle East

The oil-poor countries of Egypt, Syria, Lebanon, Jordan, and Yemen are not prospering. Their economies are in poor shape, and their governments survive by **rigging** elections and arresting their more outspoken opponents.

Of the oil-rich states, Libya has recently decided to renounce support for terrorism, to halt its development of weapons of mass destruction, and to rejoin the international community. Like Kuwait, Qatar, the United Arab Emirates, and Oman, Libya has oil reserves large enough to provide its small population with a prosperous, if undemocratic, life. Saudi Arabia has more oil, but it also has a lot more people. The Saudi royal family's monopoly on power is threatened by both pro-democratic modernizers and fundamentalist allies of al-Qaeda.

A veiled Egyptian woman walks with her daughter, April 11, 2005, in front of a building damaged by a suicide bomber in Cairo's poor Shubra neighborhood.

All Eyes on Iraq

Throughout the Middle East, governments and people are waiting to see what happens in Iraq. The country's transition to democractic government remains uncertain. Iraq's new parliament began meeting in May 2006, amid an atmosphere of insurgent violence. Whether it can bring Iraq's competing groups into harmony is unknown. If Iraq descends into civil war the consequences could affect the whole region.

A Better Future?

Some Middle Eastern governments are more democratic than others, but the region has no fully democratic countries. Israel perhaps comes the closest, but some people believe a country

Bedouin tribesmen travel the roads in ancient and modern transportation in arid surroundings on the Sinai Peninsula between Egypt and Israel.

that is dedicated to preserving a Jewish majority cannot be truly democratic. Iran offers its voters a real choice but limits what they can choose. Countries like Saudi Arabia, which deny a meaningful vote to most men and all women, are family dictatorships.

Whether real democracy would help the region is open to doubt. Islamic fundamentalists might win democratic elections, and then restrict the freedoms of those who disagreed with them.

Swinging between two different visions of the future has brought chronic instability to the region. Many Middle Easterners want the prosperity and cultural diversity that free market economies bring. Many want to preserve their traditional values and ways of life, most of which spring from their Islamic heritage. Can they find a way to have both? Or are they doomed to have neither?

Hopes of a Better Life

"The fighting in Nasiriyah went on for many days. . . . It came close to us. Artillery fire fell two meters from our house and everything broke—the windows, the glasses, and the house shook like an earthquake. There was also a lot of random shooting, which is how the old woman who lived next door was killed, by bullets coming in through the window. . . .

"I did not agree with the reason for the war. I don't believe Bush's excuse that we had illegal weapons. But I am happy to see the end of Saddam Hussein. I am a Shi'a Muslim, and he did terrible things to the Shi'as.

"But while the Americans and British talk about a 'free Iraq' it does not feel free. It will not be [free] until their [armies] have gone. Now at least we can talk about things openly. Before, if we talked about the regime, it had to be in whispers. Walls have ears, is what we used to say. So, it is a liberation."

Mukhallad al-Sinwai, a thirty-six-year-old Iraqi pharmacist, speaking soon after the overthrow of Saddam in 2003.

TIME LINE

6000 B.C. Civilization begins in the Middle East.

Fourth century B.C. Alexander the Great is the first outsider to conquer the Middle East.

Seventh century A.D. Islam founded by the Prophet Muhammad.

Seventh–eighth centuries Arab conquest of Middle East, North Africa, and Spain.

Eleventh–thirteenth centuries European Crusaders invade the Muslim Middle East.

Thirteenth century Mongol invasions of the Middle East.

Fourteenth century Ottoman Turks begin conquest of the Middle East.

1869 Suez Canal opens.

1882 British occupation of Egypt begins.

Late-nineteenth century Oil is discovered in the Middle East.

1914–1918 World War I.

1917 Balfour Declaration.

1920 Britain is given mandates to rule Palestine, Transjordan, and Iraq; France is given mandate to rule Syria (including future Lebanon).

1922 Egypt is given formal independence.

1930s Reza Shah starts the Westernization of Iran.

1932 Iraq is given formal independence.

1939–1945 World War II.

1947 UN partitions Palestine.

1947–1948 Fighting between Jews and Arabs in mandate Palestine.

1948 State of Israel is founded.

1948–1949 First Arab–Israeli War

1951–1953 Conflict between Iranian Prime Minister Mossadegh and the Western powers ends with Mossadegh's overthrow.

1952 Free Officers Movement in Egypt.

1956 Nasser's nationalization of the Suez Canal sparks the Suez Crisis.

1958 Iraqi officers overthrow pro-British regime in Baghdad.

1960 Organization of Petroleum Exporting Countries (OPEC) is founded.

1967 (June) Arab–Israeli War. (November) UN passes Resolution 242.

1968 Ba'ath party seizes power in Iraq.

1973 (October) Arab–Israeli War

1975–1991 Lebanese Civil War.

1977 Menachem Begin and hard-line Likud party win Israeli 1977 election. Egypt's President Anwar Sadat travels to Jerusalem.

1978–1996 Afghan civil wars.

1979 (January) Iranian Revolution. (March) Peace treaty between Egypt and Israel. (June) Saddam Hussein becomes president of Iraq. (December) Soviet Union intervenes in Afghanistan.

1980–1988 Iran-Iraq War.

1981 Sadat is assassinated.

1987–1988 Osama bin Laden founds al-Qaeda.

1989 Soviet Union withdraws from Afghanistan.

1990 Iraq invades Kuwait.

1991 UN coalition forces Iraq out of Kuwait.

1996 Taliban takes Afghan capital Kabul.

2001 9/11 attacks on the United States; President George W. Bush declares the War on Terror.

2003 Saddam Hussein is overthrown by United States-led invasion.

GLOSSARY

annex: to declare that a piece of land is now part of another territory

Arab League: the loose grouping of Arab countries established in 1945

Arab nationalism: the movement that advocates the development of an increasingly united Arab world

assassinated: murdered for political reasons

ayatollah: a respected religious leader among Shi'a Muslims

Ba'athism: the type of Arab nationalism that advocates pan-Arab socialism. The Ba'ath party rules Syria and used to rule Iraq until the fall of Saddam Hussein.

Canal Zone (of Suez): the strip of territory on either side of the Suez Canal

Christianity: one of the world's three major monotheistic (one-God) religions

civil war: war between different groups in the same country

clergy: officials of the church or mosque

colonial: concerning the rule of economically underdeveloped countries by economically advanced countries

Communist: an advocate of Communism, a political system in which the government owns the means of production

corrupt: involved in activities such as fraud and bribery

Crusades: the series of European military attacks on the Muslim Middle East, starting in the eleventh century and ending in the thirteenth century

Dark Ages: period of economic and cultural decline in Europe, lasting from the fifth century to the eighth century

democracy: the political system in which governments are regularly elected by the people, or a country in which this system exists

dictator: an individual who rules on his or her own, unrestricted by others

diplomacy: management of relations between countries by peaceful means, especially negotiations

economic depression: a period of time during which an economy slows down and people become poorer

economic sanctions: policies of refusing to trade with a particular country, either in one particular product or in all products, as a way of showing opposition to its policies and forcing it into compliance

ethnic: relating to different tribal, racial, cultural, or linguistic groups

exile: living, not by choice, in another country

guerrilla warfare: war involving, usually on one side only, unofficial or irregular soldiers whose attacks often include harassment and sabotage

immigration: movement of people into a country for permanent residence

insurgency: an uprising

intifada: Arabic word meaning "uprising"

Islam: one of the world's three major monotheistic (one-God) religions, founded by the Prophet Muhammad in the seventh century

Islamic fundamentalism: belief in strictly following the rules—or a particular interpretation of the rules—of Islam

Islamic Republic: government that bases its laws on Islamic law

GLOSSARY

jihad: Arabic word for "striving," often used to mean "holy war"

Judaism: one of the world's three major monotheistic (one-God) religions

land reform: change in who owns the land, usually involving taking land from the rich and distributing it among the poor

League of Nations: an international alliance, in existence from 1920 to 1946, which worked to preserve world peace

mandate: rule of a region that has been authorized by international agreement

Mesopotamian provinces: the lowlands watered by the Tigris and Euphrates rivers, now the state of Iraq

modernize: to bring up to date with current ideas and technology

Nasserism: the system of Arab nationalist ideas associated with President Nasser of Egypt

nationalist: one who is devoted to his or her own nation and puts it above all others

nationalized: took from private ownership into government ownership

oil concession: permission to drill for and extract oil

oil reserves: oil still in the ground

Ottoman Empire: empire of the Ottoman Turks, which lasted over 600 years (1299–1922), and which included all of the Middle East except Iran and the desert interior of the Arabian Peninsula

radical: (adjective) promoting far-reaching changes

refugee: person who leaves his or her own country to go to a foreign country to escape danger

Renaissance: period of European intellectual and artistic progress that began in Italy in the fourteenth century

rigging: (in elections) cheating to ensure a certain outcome

secular: not religious

security police: police concerned with the security of the government in power

shah: Iranian word for "emperor"

shipping tolls: money paid by ships for passage down a river or canal

State of the Union address: a speech given to the United States Congress each year by the country's president

terrorism: the use of violence to intimidate people for political reasons

traditionalists: (in the Middle East) those who believe that Westernization and modernization threaten traditional Islamic values

United Nations (UN): an international body set up in 1945 to promote peace and cooperation between countries

UN weapons inspectors: officials sent by the UN to make sure that a country is free of weapons of mass destruction

war on terrorism: the worldwide campaign to eliminate terrorism that began in September 2001, after the September 11 terrorist attacks on the United States

weapons of mass destruction: weapons, such as nuclear, chemical, and biological weapons, that are capable of killing thousands of people in a single blow

Westernize: to adopt Western ideas, technologies, and cultural values

FURTHER RESOURCES

Websites
BBC News: Middle East
    http://news.bbc.co.uk/1/hi/world/middle_east/
CNN International: World/Middle East
    http://edition.cnn.com/WORLD/meast/archive
History in the News: Middle East
    http://www.albany.edu/history/middle-east/
Politics: From Royalty to Democracy
    http://www.pbs.org/wgbh/globalconnections/mideast/
    themes/politics/index.html

Note to educators and parents: The publisher has carefully reviewed these Web sites to ensure that they are suitable for children. Many Web sites change frequently, however, and Gareth Stevens, Inc., cannot guarantee that a site's future contents will continue to meet our high standards of quality and educational value. Be advised that children should be closely supervised whenever they access the Internet.

Books
Margulies, Philip (editor). *The Rise of Islamic Fundamentalism* (Turning Points in World History). Greenhaven Press, 2005.

Minnis, Ivan. *Arab–Israeli Conflict*. (The Troubled World). Oxford: Heinemann Library, 2001.

Piddock, Charles. *Iran* (Nations in the News). World Almanac Library, 2006.

Suicide Bombings in Israel and Palestinian Terrorism (Terrorism in Today's World). Uschan, Michael. World Almanac Library, 2006.

ABOUT THE AUTHOR
David Downing has been writing books for adults and children about political, military, and cultural history for thirty years. He has written several books on the modern Middle East. He has lived in the United States and traveled extensively in Asia, Africa, and Latin America. He now resides in Britain.

ABOUT THE CONSULTANT
William Ochsenwald is Professor of History at Virginia Polytechnic Institute and State University. He is author of *The Middle East: A History*, a textbook now in its sixth edition. Professor Ochsenwald has also written many other books and articles dealing with the history of the Middle East.

INDEX